50 Mindful Cooking Recipes for Home

By: Kelly Johnson

Table of Contents

- Quinoa and Vegetable Stir-Fry
- Baked Salmon with Lemon and Dill
- Lentil and Spinach Soup
- Sweet Potato and Black Bean Tacos
- Lemon Garlic Roasted Chicken
- Zucchini Noodles with Pesto
- Chickpea and Vegetable Curry
- Roasted Brussels Sprouts with Balsamic Glaze
- Avocado and Tomato Salad
- Cauliflower Rice Stir-Fry
- Grilled Portobello Mushrooms with Herbs
- Mediterranean Quinoa Salad
- Spaghetti Squash with Tomato Basil Sauce
- Vegan Buddha Bowl
- Teriyaki Tofu Stir-Fry
- Caprese Salad Skewers
- Sweet Potato and Chickpea Buddha Bowl
- Garlic Parmesan Roasted Broccoli
- Cucumber and Radish Salad
- Mexican Stuffed Peppers
- Pesto Zoodles with Cherry Tomatoes
- Black Bean and Corn Salsa
- Lemon Herb Grilled Shrimp
- Eggplant Lasagna
- Roasted Asparagus with Lemon
- Greek Chickpea Salad
- Quinoa-Stuffed Bell Peppers
- Baked Cod with Herbed Butter
- Mediterranean Roasted Vegetables
- Spinach and Feta Stuffed Chicken Breast
- Butternut Squash Soup
- Roasted Red Pepper Hummus
- Garlic Ginger Soy Glazed Salmon
- Ratatouille
- Edamame and Avocado Salad

- Cauliflower Buffalo Bites
- Thai Coconut Curry Noodles
- Bruschetta with Fresh Basil
- Shrimp and Vegetable Skewers
- Roasted Sweet Potato Wedges
- Caprese Quinoa Bowl
- Lemon Dijon Baked Chicken
- Roasted Beet and Goat Cheese Salad
- Quinoa-Stuffed Acorn Squash
- Balsamic Glazed Brussels Sprouts
- Tomato Basil Mozzarella Skewers
- Mediterranean Couscous Salad
- Garlic Butter Shrimp and Broccoli
- Kale and White Bean Soup
- Ginger Sesame Tofu Stir-Fry

Quinoa and Vegetable Stir-Fry

Ingredients:

- 1 cup quinoa, rinsed and drained
- 2 cups water
- 2 tablespoons vegetable oil
- 1 onion, thinly sliced
- 2 bell peppers, thinly sliced (any color)
- 1 zucchini, thinly sliced
- 1 carrot, julienned
- 1 cup broccoli florets
- 3 cloves garlic, minced
- 1 tablespoon ginger, grated
- 1/4 cup soy sauce
- 2 tablespoons rice vinegar
- 1 tablespoon sesame oil
- 1 tablespoon honey or maple syrup
- Salt and pepper to taste
- Sesame seeds and green onions for garnish

Instructions:

In a medium saucepan, combine quinoa and water. Bring to a boil, then reduce heat to low, cover, and simmer for 15-20 minutes or until quinoa is cooked and water is absorbed. Fluff with a fork.

In a large wok or skillet, heat vegetable oil over medium-high heat. Add sliced onion and stir-fry for 2-3 minutes until softened.

Add bell peppers, zucchini, carrot, and broccoli to the wok. Stir-fry for an additional 5-7 minutes or until vegetables are tender-crisp.

Push the vegetables to the side of the wok, creating a space in the center. Add minced garlic and grated ginger to the center, stirring constantly for 1 minute until fragrant.

Combine the vegetables with the garlic and ginger. In a small bowl, whisk together soy sauce, rice vinegar, sesame oil, and honey/maple syrup. Pour the sauce over the vegetables and toss to coat evenly.

Add the cooked quinoa to the wok, tossing everything together until well combined. Season with salt and pepper to taste.

Garnish with sesame seeds and chopped green onions before serving.

Serve hot and enjoy your delicious and nutritious quinoa and vegetable stir-fry!

Baked Salmon with Lemon and Dill

Ingredients:

- 4 salmon fillets
- 2 tablespoons olive oil
- 2 tablespoons fresh lemon juice
- 2 cloves garlic, minced
- 1 tablespoon fresh dill, chopped
- Salt and pepper to taste
- Lemon slices for garnish

Instructions:

Preheat the oven to 400°F (200°C). Line a baking sheet with parchment paper or lightly grease it.

Place the salmon fillets on the prepared baking sheet, skin side down.

In a small bowl, whisk together olive oil, lemon juice, minced garlic, chopped dill, salt, and pepper.

Brush the salmon fillets with the lemon and dill mixture, ensuring they are well coated.

Place lemon slices on top of each salmon fillet for added flavor.

Bake in the preheated oven for 12-15 minutes or until the salmon easily flakes with a fork.

If desired, broil for an additional 2-3 minutes to get a golden brown color on top.

Remove from the oven and let it rest for a few minutes before serving.

Serve the baked salmon with your favorite side dishes and enjoy a flavorful and healthy meal.

Lentil and Spinach Soup

Ingredients:

- 1 cup dry green or brown lentils, rinsed and drained
- 1 tablespoon olive oil
- 1 onion, finely chopped
- 2 carrots, diced
- 2 celery stalks, diced
- 3 cloves garlic, minced
- 1 teaspoon ground cumin
- 1 teaspoon ground coriander
- 1/2 teaspoon smoked paprika
- 6 cups vegetable broth
- 1 can (14 oz) diced tomatoes, undrained
- 4 cups fresh spinach, chopped
- Salt and pepper to taste
- Lemon wedges for serving

Instructions:

In a large pot, heat olive oil over medium heat. Add chopped onions, carrots, and celery. Sauté for 5-7 minutes or until the vegetables are softened.

Add minced garlic, ground cumin, ground coriander, and smoked paprika to the pot. Stir and cook for an additional 1-2 minutes until fragrant.

Add rinsed lentils, vegetable broth, and diced tomatoes (with their juice) to the pot. Bring the mixture to a boil, then reduce heat to low, cover, and simmer for about 25-30 minutes or until the lentils are tender.

Stir in the chopped spinach and cook for an additional 3-5 minutes until the spinach is wilted.

Season the soup with salt and pepper to taste. Adjust the seasoning as needed.

Ladle the lentil and spinach soup into bowls. Serve with lemon wedges on the side for squeezing over the soup.

Enjoy a warm and hearty bowl of lentil and spinach soup, perfect for a comforting and nutritious meal.

Sweet Potato and Black Bean Tacos

Ingredients:

- 2 large sweet potatoes, peeled and diced
- 2 tablespoons olive oil
- 1 teaspoon ground cumin
- 1 teaspoon smoked paprika
- 1/2 teaspoon chili powder
- Salt and pepper to taste
- 1 can (15 oz) black beans, drained and rinsed
- 1 cup corn kernels (fresh or frozen)
- 1 red onion, finely diced
- 1/4 cup fresh cilantro, chopped
- Juice of 1 lime
- 8 small corn or flour tortillas
- Optional toppings: avocado slices, salsa, shredded lettuce, Greek yogurt

Instructions:

Preheat the oven to 400°F (200°C).

In a large bowl, toss the diced sweet potatoes with olive oil, ground cumin, smoked paprika, chili powder, salt, and pepper until evenly coated.

Spread the seasoned sweet potatoes in a single layer on a baking sheet. Roast in the preheated oven for 20-25 minutes or until the sweet potatoes are tender and lightly browned, stirring halfway through.

In a medium-sized bowl, combine black beans, corn, red onion, cilantro, and lime juice. Mix well to create the salsa.

Warm the tortillas according to package instructions.

Assemble the tacos by placing a spoonful of the roasted sweet potatoes on each tortilla. Top with the black bean and corn salsa.

Add optional toppings such as avocado slices, salsa, shredded lettuce, and a dollop of Greek yogurt.

Serve the sweet potato and black bean tacos immediately and enjoy a tasty and satisfying meatless meal.

Lemon Garlic Roasted Chicken

Ingredients:

- 4 bone-in, skin-on chicken thighs
- 2 tablespoons olive oil
- 4 cloves garlic, minced
- Zest of 1 lemon
- Juice of 1 lemon
- 1 teaspoon dried thyme
- 1 teaspoon dried rosemary
- 1 teaspoon paprika
- Salt and pepper to taste
- Fresh parsley for garnish

Instructions:

Preheat the oven to 400°F (200°C). Line a baking sheet with parchment paper or lightly grease it.

Pat the chicken thighs dry with paper towels and place them on the prepared baking sheet.

In a small bowl, whisk together olive oil, minced garlic, lemon zest, lemon juice, dried thyme, dried rosemary, paprika, salt, and pepper.

Brush the lemon-garlic mixture over each chicken thigh, ensuring they are well coated.

Bake in the preheated oven for 30-35 minutes or until the chicken reaches an internal temperature of 165°F (74°C) and the skin is crispy and golden.

If desired, broil for an additional 2-3 minutes to achieve a more golden color on top.

Remove from the oven and let the chicken rest for a few minutes.

Garnish with fresh parsley before serving.

Serve the lemon garlic roasted chicken with your favorite side dishes and enjoy a flavorful and juicy meal.

Zucchini Noodles with Pesto

Ingredients:

- 4 medium-sized zucchinis, spiralized into noodles
- 1 cup fresh basil leaves, packed
- 1/2 cup grated Parmesan cheese
- 1/3 cup pine nuts

- 2 cloves garlic, minced
- 1/2 cup extra-virgin olive oil
- Salt and pepper to taste
- Cherry tomatoes, halved, for garnish (optional)

Instructions:

In a food processor, combine basil, Parmesan cheese, pine nuts, and minced garlic. Pulse until the ingredients are finely chopped.
With the food processor running, slowly pour in the olive oil in a steady stream until the pesto reaches a smooth consistency.
Season the pesto with salt and pepper to taste. Adjust the seasoning as needed.
In a large skillet, heat a bit of olive oil over medium heat. Add the zucchini noodles and toss them gently for 2-3 minutes, just until they are heated through. Be careful not to overcook, as zucchini noodles can become too soft.
Remove the skillet from heat and add the pesto sauce to the zucchini noodles. Toss until the noodles are well coated with the pesto.
Serve the zucchini noodles with pesto in bowls, garnishing with halved cherry tomatoes if desired.
Enjoy a light and delicious meal with zucchini noodles and fresh pesto.

Chickpea and Vegetable Curry

Ingredients:

- 2 tablespoons coconut oil
- 1 large onion, finely chopped
- 3 cloves garlic, minced
- 1 tablespoon fresh ginger, grated
- 1 bell pepper, diced
- 1 zucchini, diced
- 1 carrot, sliced
- 1 cup cauliflower florets
- 1 can (15 oz) chickpeas, drained and rinsed
- 1 can (14 oz) diced tomatoes
- 1 can (14 oz) coconut milk
- 2 tablespoons curry powder
- 1 teaspoon ground turmeric
- 1 teaspoon ground cumin
- 1 teaspoon paprika

- Salt and pepper to taste
- Fresh cilantro for garnish
- Cooked rice or naan for serving

Instructions:

In a large pot or deep skillet, heat coconut oil over medium heat.
Add chopped onion, minced garlic, and grated ginger. Sauté for 2-3 minutes until the onions are softened and aromatic.
Add diced bell pepper, zucchini, carrot, and cauliflower to the pot. Cook for an additional 5-7 minutes until the vegetables start to soften.
Stir in curry powder, ground turmeric, ground cumin, and paprika. Mix well to coat the vegetables in the spices.
Pour in diced tomatoes (with their juice), coconut milk, and drained chickpeas. Season with salt and pepper to taste. Stir to combine.
Bring the curry to a simmer, then reduce the heat to low, cover, and let it simmer for 20-25 minutes, allowing the flavors to meld and the vegetables to become tender.
Taste and adjust the seasoning if needed.
Serve the chickpea and vegetable curry over cooked rice or with naan. Garnish with fresh cilantro.
Enjoy this flavorful and hearty chickpea and vegetable curry for a satisfying and plant-based meal.

Roasted Brussels Sprouts with Balsamic Glaze
Ingredients:

- 1 lb (about 500g) Brussels sprouts, trimmed and halved
- 2 tablespoons olive oil
- Salt and pepper to taste
- 2 tablespoons balsamic vinegar
- 1 tablespoon honey or maple syrup
- 1/4 cup grated Parmesan cheese (optional)
- Crushed red pepper flakes for a spicy kick (optional)

Instructions:

Preheat the oven to 400°F (200°C). Line a baking sheet with parchment paper or lightly grease it.

In a large bowl, toss the halved Brussels sprouts with olive oil, salt, and pepper until well coated.

Spread the Brussels sprouts in a single layer on the prepared baking sheet.

Roast in the preheated oven for 20-25 minutes or until the Brussels sprouts are golden brown and crispy on the edges, stirring halfway through to ensure even roasting.

While the Brussels sprouts are roasting, in a small saucepan, combine balsamic vinegar and honey/maple syrup. Bring to a simmer over medium heat and cook for 2-3 minutes or until the mixture has thickened slightly.

Once the Brussels sprouts are done roasting, transfer them to a serving dish. Drizzle the balsamic glaze over the roasted Brussels sprouts and toss to coat evenly.

If desired, sprinkle grated Parmesan cheese over the Brussels sprouts and add crushed red pepper flakes for a spicy kick.

Serve the roasted Brussels sprouts with balsamic glaze immediately, and enjoy the perfect balance of sweet, tangy, and savory flavors.

Avocado and Tomato Salad

Ingredients:

- 2 large avocados, diced
- 2 cups cherry tomatoes, halved
- 1/4 cup red onion, finely chopped
- 1/4 cup fresh cilantro, chopped
- Juice of 1 lime
- 2 tablespoons extra-virgin olive oil
- Salt and pepper to taste

Instructions:

In a large bowl, combine diced avocados, halved cherry tomatoes, chopped red onion, and chopped cilantro.

In a small bowl, whisk together the lime juice and olive oil. Pour the dressing over the avocado and tomato mixture.

Gently toss the salad to ensure all ingredients are coated with the dressing.

Season the salad with salt and pepper to taste. Adjust the seasoning as needed.

Serve the avocado and tomato salad immediately as a refreshing side dish or a light and healthy snack.

Enjoy the vibrant colors and flavors of this simple and delicious avocado and tomato salad.

Cauliflower Rice Stir-Fry

Ingredients:

- 1 medium-sized cauliflower
- 2 tablespoons sesame oil
- 1 onion, diced
- 2 carrots, diced
- 1 cup broccoli florets
- 1 bell pepper, thinly sliced
- 3 cloves garlic, minced
- 1/4 cup soy sauce
- 2 tablespoons hoisin sauce
- 1 tablespoon rice vinegar
- 1 teaspoon grated ginger
- 2 green onions, chopped (for garnish)
- Sesame seeds (for garnish)
- Salt and pepper to taste

Instructions:

Remove the leaves and stem from the cauliflower. Cut it into florets, and then pulse in a food processor until it resembles rice. Alternatively, you can use pre-packaged cauliflower rice.

In a large wok or skillet, heat sesame oil over medium-high heat.

Add diced onion, carrots, broccoli florets, and sliced bell pepper to the wok. Stir-fry for 5-7 minutes until the vegetables are tender-crisp.

Push the vegetables to one side of the wok, and add minced garlic and grated ginger to the empty space. Stir for 1-2 minutes until fragrant.

Combine the garlic and ginger with the vegetables. Add the cauliflower rice to the wok and stir to mix with the vegetables.

In a small bowl, whisk together soy sauce, hoisin sauce, and rice vinegar. Pour the sauce over the cauliflower rice and vegetables. Toss to coat evenly.

Cook for an additional 5-7 minutes, stirring occasionally, until the cauliflower rice is tender but not mushy.

Season the stir-fry with salt and pepper to taste. Adjust the seasoning as needed.

Garnish with chopped green onions and sesame seeds before serving.

Serve the cauliflower rice stir-fry as a flavorful and low-carb alternative to traditional rice stir-fry. Enjoy!

Grilled Portobello Mushrooms with Herbs
Ingredients:

- 4 large Portobello mushrooms, stems removed
- 3 tablespoons olive oil
- 2 tablespoons balsamic vinegar
- 2 cloves garlic, minced
- 1 teaspoon dried thyme
- 1 teaspoon dried rosemary
- Salt and pepper to taste
- Fresh parsley, chopped (for garnish)

Instructions:

Preheat the grill to medium-high heat.
In a small bowl, whisk together olive oil, balsamic vinegar, minced garlic, dried thyme, dried rosemary, salt, and pepper.
Brush both sides of the Portobello mushrooms with the herb-infused olive oil mixture.
Place the mushrooms on the preheated grill, gill side down. Grill for 4-5 minutes.
Flip the mushrooms and continue grilling for an additional 4-5 minutes or until they are tender and have nice grill marks.
Brush the mushrooms with any remaining olive oil mixture during the grilling process.
Remove the grilled Portobello mushrooms from the grill and transfer them to a serving plate.
Garnish with fresh chopped parsley before serving.
Serve the grilled Portobello mushrooms as a tasty and satisfying appetizer or as a side dish to complement your main course. Enjoy the savory flavors and meaty texture!

Mediterranean Quinoa Salad

Ingredients:

For the Salad:

- 1 cup quinoa, rinsed and cooked according to package instructions
- 1 cucumber, diced
- 1 cup cherry tomatoes, halved

- 1/2 red onion, finely chopped
- 1/2 cup Kalamata olives, sliced
- 1/2 cup feta cheese, crumbled
- 1/4 cup fresh parsley, chopped
- 1/4 cup fresh mint, chopped

For the Dressing:

- 1/4 cup extra virgin olive oil
- 2 tablespoons red wine vinegar
- 1 clove garlic, minced
- 1 teaspoon dried oregano
- Salt and pepper to taste

Instructions:

Cook quinoa according to package instructions. Once cooked, let it cool to room temperature.

In a large bowl, combine the cooked quinoa, diced cucumber, cherry tomatoes, chopped red onion, sliced Kalamata olives, crumbled feta cheese, chopped parsley, and chopped mint.

In a small bowl or jar, whisk together the extra virgin olive oil, red wine vinegar, minced garlic, dried oregano, salt, and pepper to create the dressing.

Pour the dressing over the quinoa and vegetable mixture. Toss everything together until well combined, ensuring that the salad is evenly coated with the dressing.

Taste and adjust the seasoning if needed. You can add more salt, pepper, or herbs according to your preference.

Refrigerate the salad for at least 30 minutes to allow the flavors to meld and the salad to chill.

Before serving, give the salad a final toss and garnish with additional fresh herbs if desired.

Serve chilled and enjoy your refreshing Mediterranean Quinoa Salad!

Feel free to customize the recipe by adding other Mediterranean ingredients like artichoke hearts, roasted red peppers, or capers. This salad is not only tasty but also a great option for a healthy and satisfying meal or side dish.

Spaghetti Squash with Tomato Basil Sauce

Ingredients:

For the Spaghetti Squash:

- 1 medium-sized spaghetti squash
- Olive oil
- Salt and pepper to taste

For the Tomato Basil Sauce:

- 2 tablespoons olive oil
- 3 cloves garlic, minced
- 1 can (28 oz) crushed tomatoes
- 1 teaspoon dried oregano
- 1 teaspoon dried basil
- Salt and pepper to taste
- Red pepper flakes (optional, for some heat)
- Fresh basil leaves, for garnish
- Grated Parmesan cheese, for serving

Instructions:

For the Spaghetti Squash:

> Preheat the oven to 375°F (190°C).
> Cut the spaghetti squash in half lengthwise and scoop out the seeds.
> Drizzle the cut sides of the squash with olive oil, and season with salt and pepper.
> Place the squash, cut side down, on a baking sheet lined with parchment paper.
> Bake in the preheated oven for about 35-45 minutes or until the squash is tender and easily pierced with a fork.
> Once cooked, use a fork to scrape the flesh of the squash into spaghetti-like strands.

For the Tomato Basil Sauce:

> In a large skillet, heat olive oil over medium heat. Add minced garlic and sauté until fragrant.
> Pour in the crushed tomatoes, dried oregano, dried basil, salt, pepper, and red pepper flakes (if using). Stir to combine.

Simmer the sauce for about 15-20 minutes, allowing the flavors to meld and the sauce to thicken.
Taste and adjust the seasoning as needed. If you prefer a smoother sauce, you can use an immersion blender to puree it.

Assembling:

Spoon the tomato basil sauce over the spaghetti squash strands.
Garnish with fresh basil leaves and grated Parmesan cheese.
Serve immediately and enjoy your Spaghetti Squash with Tomato Basil Sauce!

This dish is a great way to enjoy the flavors of traditional spaghetti and tomato sauce while incorporating the health benefits of spaghetti squash. Feel free to add some cooked protein such as grilled chicken or shrimp if you'd like to make it a heartier meal.
Vegan Buddha Bowl

Ingredients:

For the Buddha Bowl:

- 1 cup cooked quinoa or brown rice
- 1 cup chickpeas, drained and rinsed
- 1 cup cherry tomatoes, halved
- 1 cucumber, sliced
- 1 avocado, sliced
- 1 cup shredded carrots
- 2 cups baby spinach or kale, chopped
- Sesame seeds or hemp seeds for garnish (optional)

For the Tahini Dressing:

- 1/4 cup tahini
- 2 tablespoons lemon juice
- 2 tablespoons water (adjust for desired consistency)
- 1 clove garlic, minced
- 1 tablespoon maple syrup or agave nectar
- Salt and pepper to taste

Instructions:

For the Buddha Bowl:

- Cook quinoa or brown rice according to package instructions.
- In a large bowl, arrange the cooked quinoa or brown rice, chickpeas, cherry tomatoes, cucumber slices, avocado slices, shredded carrots, and chopped baby spinach or kale in separate sections.
- Sprinkle sesame seeds or hemp seeds over the bowl for added texture and nutrition.

For the Tahini Dressing:

- In a small bowl, whisk together tahini, lemon juice, water, minced garlic, maple syrup or agave nectar, salt, and pepper. Adjust the water quantity to achieve your desired dressing consistency.
- Taste the dressing and adjust the flavor by adding more lemon juice, salt, or sweetener if necessary.

Assembling:

- Drizzle the tahini dressing over the ingredients in the Buddha Bowl.
- Toss everything together just before serving, ensuring the dressing evenly coats the vegetables, grains, and legumes.
- Garnish with additional sesame seeds or hemp seeds if desired.
- Serve immediately and enjoy your Vegan Buddha Bowl!

Feel free to customize your Buddha Bowl by adding other favorite vegetables, roasted sweet potatoes, hummus, or any plant-based protein of your choice. The key is to create a balanced and visually appealing bowl with a variety of textures and flavors.

Teriyaki Tofu Stir-Fry

Ingredients:

For the Teriyaki Sauce:

- 1/4 cup soy sauce or tamari (for a gluten-free option)
- 2 tablespoons rice vinegar
- 2 tablespoons maple syrup or agave nectar
- 1 clove garlic, minced
- 1 teaspoon fresh ginger, grated
- 1 tablespoon cornstarch mixed with 2 tablespoons water (for thickening)

For the Stir-Fry:

- 1 block (14-16 oz) extra-firm tofu, pressed and cubed
- 2 tablespoons vegetable oil
- 1 bell pepper, sliced
- 1 broccoli crown, cut into florets
- 1 carrot, julienned
- 1 cup snap peas, trimmed
- 3 green onions, sliced (for garnish)
- Sesame seeds for garnish (optional)
- Cooked brown rice or noodles for serving

Instructions:

For the Teriyaki Sauce:

In a small saucepan, combine soy sauce or tamari, rice vinegar, maple syrup or agave nectar, minced garlic, and grated ginger.

Heat the sauce over medium heat, bringing it to a simmer.

In a small bowl, mix the cornstarch with water to create a slurry. Slowly whisk the slurry into the sauce, stirring continuously.

Continue to simmer the sauce until it thickens. Once thickened, remove it from heat and set aside.

For the Tofu Stir-Fry:

Press the tofu to remove excess water. Cut the tofu into cubes.

Heat 1 tablespoon of vegetable oil in a large skillet or wok over medium-high heat. Add the tofu cubes and cook until golden brown on all sides. Remove the tofu from the skillet and set aside.

In the same skillet, add another tablespoon of oil. Stir in the sliced bell pepper, broccoli florets, julienned carrot, and snap peas. Stir-fry the vegetables until they are crisp-tender but still vibrant.

Add the cooked tofu back to the skillet with the vegetables.

Pour the teriyaki sauce over the tofu and vegetables. Stir everything together, making sure the tofu and vegetables are well coated in the sauce.

Cook for an additional 2-3 minutes, allowing the flavors to meld.

Serve the Teriyaki Tofu Stir-Fry over cooked brown rice or noodles.

Garnish with sliced green onions and sesame seeds if desired.

Enjoy your delicious Teriyaki Tofu Stir-Fry! This dish is not only flavorful but also packed with protein and a variety of colorful vegetables. Adjust the sauce ingredients to your taste preferences, and feel free to add other favorite vegetables like mushrooms, baby corn, or water chestnuts.

Caprese Salad Skewers

Ingredients:

- Cherry tomatoes
- Fresh mozzarella balls (bocconcini)
- Fresh basil leaves
- Balsamic glaze (store-bought or homemade)
- Extra virgin olive oil
- Salt and pepper to taste
- Wooden or bamboo skewers

Instructions:

Prepare Ingredients:
- Rinse the cherry tomatoes and pat them dry.
- Drain the fresh mozzarella balls if they are stored in liquid.
- Wash and dry the fresh basil leaves.

Assemble Skewers:
- Take a wooden or bamboo skewer and thread a cherry tomato onto it.
- Follow with a fresh basil leaf folded or rolled up.
- Add a mozzarella ball onto the skewer.
- Repeat the process until you have a set of Caprese Salad Skewers.

Arrange on a Platter:
- Place the assembled skewers on a serving platter.

Drizzle with Olive Oil and Balsamic Glaze:
- Drizzle extra virgin olive oil over the skewers.
- Drizzle balsamic glaze over the top for added flavor and a decorative touch.

Season with Salt and Pepper:
- Sprinkle a bit of salt and pepper over the skewers to enhance the flavors.

Serve:
- Arrange the Caprese Salad Skewers on a platter and serve them as a refreshing and elegant appetizer.

Optional Variations:

- **Prosciutto-Wrapped:** For a variation, you can wrap each mozzarella ball with a slice of prosciutto before threading it onto the skewer.
- **Fruit Addition:** Add a sweet touch by alternating cherry tomatoes with small, fresh fruit such as strawberries or melon cubes.
- **Grilled Option:** If you prefer a warm appetizer, you can grill the assembled skewers briefly on each side to slightly melt the mozzarella.

Caprese Salad Skewers are perfect for gatherings, parties, or as a light and flavorful starter. They capture the essence of a traditional Caprese salad in a convenient and easy-to-eat format.
Sweet Potato and Chickpea Buddha Bowl

Ingredients:

For the Sweet Potatoes and Chickpeas:

- 2 medium sweet potatoes, peeled and diced
- 1 can (15 oz) chickpeas, drained and rinsed
- 2 tablespoons olive oil
- 1 teaspoon smoked paprika
- 1 teaspoon cumin
- 1/2 teaspoon garlic powder
- Salt and pepper to taste

For the Quinoa:

- 1 cup quinoa, rinsed
- 2 cups vegetable broth or water

For the Bowl Assembly:

- Baby spinach or kale leaves
- Avocado slices
- Cherry tomatoes, halved
- Cucumber, sliced
- Red cabbage, thinly sliced
- Tahini dressing (store-bought or homemade)

Instructions:

For the Sweet Potatoes and Chickpeas:

Preheat the oven to 400°F (200°C).

In a bowl, toss the diced sweet potatoes and chickpeas with olive oil, smoked paprika, cumin, garlic powder, salt, and pepper until well coated.

Spread the sweet potatoes and chickpeas on a baking sheet in a single layer.

Roast in the preheated oven for about 25-30 minutes or until the sweet potatoes are tender and the chickpeas are crispy.

For the Quinoa:

In a medium saucepan, combine the quinoa and vegetable broth or water.

Bring to a boil, then reduce the heat to low, cover, and simmer for 15-20 minutes or until the quinoa is cooked and the liquid is absorbed.

Fluff the quinoa with a fork and set aside.

Bowl Assembly:

In each bowl, start with a base of baby spinach or kale leaves.

Add a portion of cooked quinoa to one side of the bowl.

Arrange the roasted sweet potatoes and chickpeas on the other side.

Garnish the bowl with avocado slices, halved cherry tomatoes, cucumber slices, and thinly sliced red cabbage.

Drizzle with tahini dressing or your favorite dressing.

Repeat for each bowl, and serve immediately.

Enjoy your delicious and nutritious Sweet Potato and Chickpea Buddha Bowl! This versatile dish can be customized with your favorite vegetables, and the combination of flavors and textures makes it a satisfying and wholesome meal.

Garlic Parmesan Roasted Broccoli

Ingredients:

- 1 lb (about 450g) fresh broccoli, washed and cut into florets
- 3 tablespoons olive oil
- 4 cloves garlic, minced
- 1/2 cup grated Parmesan cheese
- 1 teaspoon dried oregano
- Salt and black pepper to taste
- Lemon wedges for serving (optional)

Instructions:

Preheat the Oven:
- Preheat your oven to 425°F (220°C).

Prepare Broccoli:
- Wash the broccoli and cut it into florets. Make sure the florets are similar in size for even roasting.

Mix the Ingredients:
- In a large mixing bowl, combine the broccoli florets with olive oil, minced garlic, grated Parmesan cheese, dried oregano, salt, and black pepper. Toss the broccoli until it is evenly coated with the mixture.

Roast in the Oven:
- Spread the broccoli mixture on a baking sheet in a single layer, making sure not to overcrowd the pan.
- Roast in the preheated oven for about 20-25 minutes or until the broccoli is tender and the edges are golden and crispy. You can toss the broccoli halfway through the cooking time for even roasting.

Serve:
- Remove the roasted broccoli from the oven and transfer it to a serving dish.
- Optionally, squeeze some fresh lemon juice over the top for a burst of citrus flavor.

Garnish:
- Garnish the Garlic Parmesan Roasted Broccoli with additional grated Parmesan cheese if desired.

Serve Warm:
- Serve the roasted broccoli warm as a delicious side dish for any meal.

Enjoy your Garlic Parmesan Roasted Broccoli as a tasty and nutritious side dish! This recipe is a great way to elevate the flavors of plain broccoli and make it a favorite among both kids and adults.

Cucumber and Radish Salad

Ingredients:

- 2 large cucumbers, thinly sliced
- 1 bunch of radishes, thinly sliced

- 1/4 red onion, thinly sliced (optional)
- 1/4 cup fresh dill, chopped
- 2 tablespoons olive oil
- 2 tablespoons white wine vinegar or apple cider vinegar
- Salt and pepper to taste
- Optional: Feta cheese crumbles for garnish

Instructions:

Prepare Vegetables:
- Wash the cucumbers, radishes, and dill. Trim the ends of the cucumbers and radishes.
- Thinly slice the cucumbers and radishes. If you're using red onion, thinly slice it as well.

Combine Vegetables:
- In a large bowl, combine the sliced cucumbers, radishes, and red onion (if using).

Add Fresh Dill:
- Add the chopped fresh dill to the bowl with the vegetables.

Prepare Dressing:
- In a small bowl, whisk together the olive oil and white wine vinegar.

Dress the Salad:
- Pour the dressing over the cucumber, radish, and dill mixture.

Season:
- Season the salad with salt and pepper to taste. Toss everything gently to ensure even coating.

Optional Garnish:
- If desired, garnish the salad with feta cheese crumbles for added flavor.

Chill (Optional):
- Refrigerate the salad for about 15-30 minutes before serving to allow the flavors to meld. This step is optional but can enhance the overall taste.

Serve:
- Serve the Cucumber and Radish Salad as a refreshing side dish alongside your favorite main course.

Enjoy this light and crunchy salad that showcases the natural flavors of cucumbers and radishes with a hint of dill. It's perfect for picnics, barbecues, or as a quick and healthy side for any meal.

Mexican Stuffed Peppers

Ingredients:

For the Stuffed Peppers:

- 4 large bell peppers, halved and seeds removed
- 1 lb (450g) ground beef or turkey
- 1 cup cooked rice (white or brown)
- 1 cup black beans, drained and rinsed
- 1 cup corn kernels (fresh, frozen, or canned)
- 1 cup diced tomatoes
- 1 cup shredded Mexican blend cheese
- 1 small onion, finely chopped
- 2 cloves garlic, minced
- 1 tablespoon chili powder
- 1 teaspoon ground cumin
- 1 teaspoon paprika
- Salt and pepper to taste

For Topping (Optional):

- Chopped fresh cilantro
- Salsa
- Sour cream
- Avocado slices

Instructions:

Preheat the Oven:
- Preheat your oven to 375°F (190°C).

Prepare the Peppers:
- Cut the bell peppers in half, removing the seeds and membranes. Place them in a baking dish.

Cook the Ground Meat:
- In a large skillet, cook the ground beef or turkey over medium heat until browned. Drain any excess fat.

Saute Vegetables:
- Add chopped onions and minced garlic to the skillet with the cooked meat. Cook until the onions are translucent.

Season the Mixture:

- Stir in chili powder, ground cumin, paprika, salt, and pepper. Mix well to coat the meat and vegetables with the spices.

Combine Ingredients:
- In a large mixing bowl, combine the cooked meat mixture, cooked rice, black beans, corn, diced tomatoes, and half of the shredded cheese.

Stuff the Peppers:
- Fill each bell pepper half with the mixture, pressing it down gently.

Bake:
- Sprinkle the remaining shredded cheese over the stuffed peppers.
- Cover the baking dish with aluminum foil and bake in the preheated oven for about 25-30 minutes, or until the peppers are tender.

Serve:
- Remove from the oven and let it cool slightly. Serve the Mexican Stuffed Peppers with your choice of toppings such as chopped cilantro, salsa, sour cream, or avocado slices.

Enjoy your delicious and hearty Mexican Stuffed Peppers! This versatile dish can be customized with your favorite ingredients and toppings for a flavorful meal.

Pesto Zoodles with Cherry Tomatoes

Ingredients:

For the Pesto:
- 2 cups fresh basil leaves, packed
- 1/2 cup grated Parmesan cheese
- 1/3 cup pine nuts or walnuts
- 2 cloves garlic, minced
- 1/2 cup extra virgin olive oil
- Salt and pepper to taste
- Juice of half a lemon (optional)

For the Zoodles:
- 4 medium-sized zucchinis
- 1 tablespoon olive oil
- 1 pint cherry tomatoes, halved
- Salt and pepper to taste
- Red pepper flakes (optional, for some heat)

- Additional Parmesan cheese for garnish

Instructions:

For the Pesto:

Prepare Ingredients:
- In a food processor, combine the fresh basil, grated Parmesan cheese, pine nuts or walnuts, and minced garlic.

Blend:
- Pulse the ingredients while slowly drizzling in the olive oil until the pesto reaches your desired consistency.

Season:
- Season with salt and pepper to taste. Add lemon juice if desired for a citrusy kick.

Set Aside:
- Transfer the pesto to a bowl and set it aside.

For the Zoodles:

Make Zoodles:
- Using a spiralizer, create zucchini noodles (zoodles) from the zucchinis.

Cook Zoodles:
- Heat olive oil in a large skillet over medium heat. Add the zoodles and sauté for 2-3 minutes, just until they are slightly softened but still have a bit of crunch.

Add Cherry Tomatoes:
- Add the halved cherry tomatoes to the skillet and sauté for an additional 1-2 minutes until the tomatoes are slightly softened.

Combine with Pesto:
- Add the prepared pesto to the skillet with zoodles and cherry tomatoes. Toss everything together until well coated.

Season:
- Season with salt, pepper, and red pepper flakes (if using) to taste.

Serve:
- Serve the Pesto Zoodles with Cherry Tomatoes in bowls, garnished with additional Parmesan cheese if desired.

Enjoy your light and delicious Pesto Zoodles with Cherry Tomatoes! This dish is not only tasty but also low-carb and full of fresh, vibrant flavors.

Black Bean and Corn Salsa

Ingredients:

- 1 can (15 oz) black beans, drained and rinsed
- 1 cup frozen corn, thawed (or use fresh corn kernels)
- 1 cup cherry tomatoes, diced
- 1/2 red onion, finely chopped
- 1/4 cup fresh cilantro, chopped
- 1 jalapeño, seeds removed and finely chopped (optional, for some heat)
- 1 avocado, diced
- Juice of 2 limes
- 2 tablespoons extra virgin olive oil
- Salt and pepper to taste
- Tortilla chips for serving

Instructions:

Prepare Ingredients:
- Drain and rinse the black beans.
- Thaw the frozen corn or use fresh corn kernels.
- Dice the cherry tomatoes, finely chop the red onion, and chop the fresh cilantro.

Combine Ingredients:
- In a large bowl, combine the black beans, corn, cherry tomatoes, red onion, cilantro, and chopped jalapeño (if using).

Add Avocado:
- Gently fold in the diced avocado to avoid mashing it.

Prepare Dressing:
- In a small bowl, whisk together the lime juice, extra virgin olive oil, salt, and pepper.

Combine with Dressing:
- Pour the dressing over the black bean and corn mixture. Toss everything together until well coated.

Chill (Optional):
- Refrigerate the salsa for about 30 minutes before serving to allow the flavors to meld. This step is optional but can enhance the taste.

Serve:
- Serve the Black Bean and Corn Salsa with tortilla chips as a dip or as a topping for tacos, grilled chicken, or fish.

Enjoy your fresh and flavorful Black Bean and Corn Salsa! This dish is not only a great appetizer but also a colorful and nutritious addition to various meals. Adjust the spice level by adding more or less jalapeño according to your preference.

Lemon Herb Grilled Shrimp

Ingredients:

- 1 pound large shrimp, peeled and deveined
- 3 tablespoons olive oil
- Zest of 1 lemon
- Juice of 1 lemon
- 2 cloves garlic, minced
- 1 teaspoon dried oregano
- 1 teaspoon dried thyme
- 1 teaspoon paprika
- Salt and black pepper to taste
- Fresh parsley, chopped, for garnish
- Lemon wedges for serving

Instructions:

Marinate Shrimp:
- In a bowl, combine olive oil, lemon zest, lemon juice, minced garlic, dried oregano, dried thyme, paprika, salt, and black pepper. Whisk the ingredients together.

Coat Shrimp:
- Add the peeled and deveined shrimp to the marinade, making sure each shrimp is well coated. Marinate for at least 15-30 minutes in the refrigerator.

Preheat Grill:
- Preheat your grill to medium-high heat.

Skewer Shrimp (Optional):
- If using skewers, thread the marinated shrimp onto skewers for easier grilling.

Grill Shrimp:

- Grill the shrimp for 2-3 minutes per side or until they are opaque and have nice grill marks. Be careful not to overcook as shrimp can become rubbery.

Garnish:
- Remove the shrimp from the grill and garnish with chopped fresh parsley.

Serve:
- Serve the Lemon Herb Grilled Shrimp hot with lemon wedges on the side.

Enjoy your Lemon Herb Grilled Shrimp as a tasty appetizer or as part of a light summer meal. You can serve them on their own, over a bed of greens, or alongside your favorite side dishes. Adjust the seasoning to your liking and feel free to experiment with additional herbs or spices to suit your taste preferences.

Eggplant Lasagna

Ingredients:

For the Eggplant:

- 2 large eggplants, sliced lengthwise into 1/4-inch thick slices
- Salt, for sprinkling
- Olive oil for brushing

For the Filling:

- 1 pound ground beef or ground turkey
- 1 onion, finely chopped
- 3 cloves garlic, minced
- 1 can (14 oz) crushed tomatoes
- 1 can (14 oz) tomato sauce
- 1 teaspoon dried oregano
- 1 teaspoon dried basil
- Salt and black pepper to taste

For the Cheese Mixture:

- 2 cups ricotta cheese
- 1 cup grated Parmesan cheese
- 1 egg
- 1 tablespoon fresh basil, chopped

- Salt and black pepper to taste

For Assembly:

- 2 cups shredded mozzarella cheese
- Fresh basil leaves for garnish (optional)

Instructions:

For the Eggplant:

Prep Eggplant:
- Preheat the oven to 375°F (190°C).
- Place the eggplant slices on a baking sheet and sprinkle them with salt. Let them sit for about 15-20 minutes to release excess moisture.

Brush with Olive Oil:
- Rinse the salt off the eggplant slices and pat them dry with paper towels. Brush both sides of each slice with olive oil.

Roast Eggplant:
- Arrange the eggplant slices on the baking sheet in a single layer. Roast in the preheated oven for about 15-20 minutes or until they are tender and slightly golden. Set aside.

For the Filling:

Cook Meat Mixture:
- In a large skillet, cook the ground beef or turkey over medium heat until browned. Drain excess fat.

Add Onion and Garlic:
- Add chopped onion and minced garlic to the skillet. Cook until the onion is translucent.

Add Tomato Sauce:
- Stir in crushed tomatoes, tomato sauce, dried oregano, dried basil, salt, and black pepper. Simmer for about 15-20 minutes to allow the flavors to meld.

For the Cheese Mixture:

Combine Ingredients:
- In a bowl, mix together ricotta cheese, grated Parmesan cheese, egg, fresh basil, salt, and black pepper.

For Assembly:

Layer Ingredients:
- In a greased baking dish, layer the components: start with a layer of eggplant slices, followed by a layer of the meat sauce, a layer of the cheese mixture, and a sprinkle of shredded mozzarella. Repeat until all ingredients are used, finishing with a layer of shredded mozzarella on top.

Bake:
- Bake in the preheated oven for about 30-40 minutes or until the cheese is bubbly and golden brown.

Rest and Serve:
- Let the eggplant lasagna rest for about 10 minutes before slicing. Garnish with fresh basil leaves if desired.

Enjoy your Eggplant Lasagna, a tasty and satisfying dish that's perfect for those looking for a low-carb or gluten-free alternative to traditional lasagna.

Roasted Asparagus with Lemon

Ingredients:

- 1 bunch of fresh asparagus
- 2 tablespoons olive oil
- Zest of 1 lemon
- Juice of 1 lemon
- Salt and black pepper to taste
- Grated Parmesan cheese (optional, for garnish)

Instructions:

Preheat the Oven:
- Preheat your oven to 400°F (200°C).

Prepare Asparagus:
- Wash the asparagus and trim the tough ends. You can do this by snapping off the woody ends or cutting them with a knife.

Coat with Olive Oil:
- Place the trimmed asparagus on a baking sheet. Drizzle olive oil over the asparagus and toss them to ensure they are evenly coated.

Zest Lemon:
- Zest the lemon using a fine grater or a lemon zester.

Season:

- Sprinkle lemon zest over the asparagus. Squeeze the lemon to extract the juice and drizzle it over the asparagus. Season with salt and black pepper to taste.

Toss:
- Toss the asparagus to evenly distribute the oil, lemon zest, and juice.

Roast in the Oven:
- Roast the asparagus in the preheated oven for about 12-15 minutes or until they are tender and slightly browned.

Optional Garnish:
- If desired, sprinkle grated Parmesan cheese over the roasted asparagus during the last 5 minutes of cooking, allowing it to melt and become slightly crispy.

Serve:
- Transfer the roasted asparagus to a serving dish and serve immediately.

Enjoy your Roasted Asparagus with Lemon as a vibrant and nutritious side dish. The combination of the roasted asparagus and the bright lemon flavor creates a delightful and refreshing dish that pairs well with a variety of main courses.

Greek Chickpea Salad

Ingredients:

For the Salad:

- 2 cans (15 oz each) chickpeas, drained and rinsed
- 1 cucumber, diced
- 1 cup cherry tomatoes, halved
- 1 red bell pepper, diced
- 1 yellow bell pepper, diced
- 1/2 red onion, finely chopped
- 1/2 cup Kalamata olives, pitted and sliced
- 1/2 cup crumbled feta cheese
- Fresh parsley, chopped, for garnish

For the Dressing:

- 1/4 cup extra virgin olive oil
- 2 tablespoons red wine vinegar

- 1 teaspoon dried oregano
- 1 clove garlic, minced
- Salt and black pepper to taste
- Juice of 1 lemon (optional)

Instructions:

For the Salad:

Prepare Chickpeas:
- Rinse and drain the chickpeas thoroughly.

Chop Vegetables:
- Dice the cucumber, red and yellow bell peppers. Halve the cherry tomatoes. Finely chop the red onion.

Assemble Salad:
- In a large salad bowl, combine the chickpeas, diced cucumber, cherry tomatoes, red and yellow bell peppers, chopped red onion, sliced Kalamata olives, and crumbled feta cheese.

For the Dressing:

Prepare Dressing:
- In a small bowl, whisk together the extra virgin olive oil, red wine vinegar, dried oregano, minced garlic, salt, and black pepper. Add the juice of 1 lemon if desired for extra freshness.

Combine with Salad:
- Pour the dressing over the salad ingredients.

Toss Gently:
- Gently toss the salad until all ingredients are well coated with the dressing.

Chill (Optional):
- Refrigerate the Greek Chickpea Salad for about 30 minutes before serving to allow the flavors to meld. This step is optional but can enhance the taste.

Garnish:
- Garnish the salad with freshly chopped parsley.

Serve:
- Serve the Greek Chickpea Salad as a refreshing and satisfying dish on its own or as a side to your favorite grilled meats or seafood.

Enjoy this vibrant and healthy Greek Chickpea Salad that's bursting with Mediterranean flavors! Feel free to customize the ingredients or add other vegetables like artichoke hearts, diced cucumber, or avocado to suit your taste preferences.

Quinoa-Stuffed Bell Peppers

Ingredients:

For the Quinoa Stuffing:

- 1 cup quinoa, rinsed
- 2 cups vegetable broth or water
- 1 tablespoon olive oil
- 1 onion, finely chopped
- 2 cloves garlic, minced
- 1 zucchini, diced
- 1 red bell pepper, diced
- 1 yellow bell pepper, diced
- 1 cup corn kernels (fresh, frozen, or canned)
- 1 can (15 oz) black beans, drained and rinsed
- 1 teaspoon ground cumin
- 1 teaspoon chili powder
- Salt and black pepper to taste
- Juice of 1 lime

For the Bell Peppers:

- 4 large bell peppers, halved and seeds removed
- Olive oil for brushing
- Salt and black pepper to taste

Optional Toppings:

- Shredded cheese (cheddar, Monterey Jack, or your choice)
- Fresh cilantro, chopped
- Avocado slices
- Salsa or hot sauce

Instructions:

For the Quinoa Stuffing:

Cook Quinoa:
- In a saucepan, combine quinoa and vegetable broth (or water). Bring to a boil, then reduce heat, cover, and simmer for about 15 minutes or until quinoa is cooked and liquid is absorbed.

Saute Vegetables:
- In a large skillet, heat olive oil over medium heat. Add chopped onion and garlic, sauté until softened.

Add Zucchini and Peppers:
- Add diced zucchini, red bell pepper, and yellow bell pepper to the skillet. Cook until vegetables are tender.

Combine with Quinoa:
- Stir in cooked quinoa, black beans, corn, ground cumin, chili powder, salt, black pepper, and lime juice. Mix well to combine.

For the Bell Peppers:

Prepare Bell Peppers:
- Preheat the oven to 375°F (190°C).
- Cut the bell peppers in half lengthwise and remove seeds and membranes.

Brush with Olive Oil:
- Brush the outside of each pepper half with olive oil and sprinkle with salt and black pepper.

Stuff Peppers:
- Fill each bell pepper half with the quinoa stuffing mixture.

Bake:
- Place the stuffed peppers in a baking dish. Cover with foil and bake for about 25-30 minutes, or until the peppers are tender.

Optional Cheese Topping:
- If desired, remove the foil, sprinkle shredded cheese over each stuffed pepper, and bake for an additional 5-7 minutes, or until the cheese is melted and bubbly.

Garnish and Serve:
- Garnish with chopped cilantro and serve with avocado slices and salsa or hot sauce.

Enjoy your delicious and wholesome quinoa-stuffed bell peppers! This dish is not only visually appealing but also packed with protein, fiber, and a variety of flavors.

Baked Cod with Herbed Butter

Ingredients:

For the Herbed Butter:

- 1/2 cup (1 stick) unsalted butter, softened
- 2 tablespoons fresh parsley, finely chopped
- 1 tablespoon fresh chives, finely chopped
- 1 teaspoon fresh dill, chopped
- 1 clove garlic, minced
- Zest of 1 lemon
- Salt and black pepper to taste

For the Baked Cod:

- 4 cod fillets
- Olive oil for drizzling
- Salt and black pepper to taste
- Lemon wedges for serving
- Fresh parsley, chopped, for garnish

Instructions:

For the Herbed Butter:

Prepare Herbed Butter:
- In a bowl, combine softened butter with chopped parsley, chives, dill, minced garlic, lemon zest, salt, and black pepper. Mix well until all the ingredients are evenly incorporated.

Shape into a Log (Optional):
- Optionally, you can shape the herbed butter into a log using plastic wrap and refrigerate it until firm. This makes it easier to slice and serve over the baked cod.

For the Baked Cod:

Preheat the Oven:
- Preheat your oven to 400°F (200°C).

Prepare Cod Fillets:
- Pat the cod fillets dry with paper towels. Place them on a baking sheet lined with parchment paper.

Season Cod:
- Drizzle olive oil over the cod fillets. Season with salt and black pepper to taste.

Spread Herbed Butter:
- Spoon a generous portion of the herbed butter over each cod fillet, spreading it evenly.

Bake:
- Bake in the preheated oven for about 12-15 minutes, or until the cod is opaque and flakes easily with a fork.

Broil (Optional):
- If you prefer a golden brown crust, you can broil the cod for an additional 1-2 minutes at the end of the baking time.

Garnish and Serve:
- Remove the baked cod from the oven and garnish with chopped fresh parsley. Serve hot with lemon wedges on the side.

Enjoy your Baked Cod with Herbed Butter – a delightful dish that combines the mild flavor of cod with the aromatic richness of the herbed butter. This recipe is quick to prepare, making it perfect for a delicious and hassle-free meal.

Mediterranean Roasted Vegetables

Ingredients:

- 1 large eggplant, diced
- 2 medium zucchinis, sliced
- 1 red bell pepper, sliced
- 1 yellow bell pepper, sliced
- 1 red onion, thinly sliced
- 1 pint cherry tomatoes, halved
- 4 cloves garlic, minced
- 1/4 cup extra virgin olive oil
- 1 teaspoon dried oregano
- 1 teaspoon dried thyme
- 1 teaspoon dried rosemary
- Salt and black pepper to taste
- Juice of 1 lemon
- Fresh parsley, chopped, for garnish

Instructions:

Preheat the Oven:

- Preheat your oven to 425°F (220°C).

Prepare Vegetables:
- In a large mixing bowl, combine diced eggplant, sliced zucchinis, sliced red and yellow bell peppers, thinly sliced red onion, and halved cherry tomatoes.

Season Vegetables:
- Add minced garlic, extra virgin olive oil, dried oregano, dried thyme, dried rosemary, salt, and black pepper to the bowl. Toss the vegetables until they are well coated with the seasoning.

Roast in the Oven:
- Spread the seasoned vegetables on a large baking sheet in a single layer.
- Roast in the preheated oven for about 25-30 minutes, or until the vegetables are tender and slightly caramelized. You can toss them halfway through the cooking time for even roasting.

Finish with Lemon Juice:
- Squeeze the juice of one lemon over the roasted vegetables and gently toss to combine.

Garnish:
- Garnish the Mediterranean Roasted Vegetables with freshly chopped parsley.

Serve:
- Serve the roasted vegetables as a side dish, over cooked quinoa or couscous, or as a topping for salads.

Enjoy your Mediterranean Roasted Vegetables! This dish is not only vibrant and delicious but also a great way to incorporate a variety of vegetables into your diet. Feel free to customize the herb seasoning based on your preferences.

Spinach and Feta Stuffed Chicken Breast

Ingredients:

For the Stuffed Chicken:
- 4 boneless, skinless chicken breasts
- Salt and black pepper to taste
- 1 tablespoon olive oil

For the Spinach and Feta Filling:

- 2 cups fresh spinach, chopped
- 1 cup crumbled feta cheese
- 1/4 cup sun-dried tomatoes, chopped (optional)
- 2 cloves garlic, minced
- 1 tablespoon olive oil
- Salt and black pepper to taste

For the Herb Seasoning (Optional):

- 1 teaspoon dried oregano
- 1 teaspoon dried thyme
- 1 teaspoon dried rosemary

Instructions:

For the Spinach and Feta Filling:

Prepare Spinach:

- In a skillet, heat 1 tablespoon of olive oil over medium heat. Add minced garlic and sauté for about 1 minute until fragrant.

Add Spinach:

- Add chopped fresh spinach to the skillet. Cook for 2-3 minutes until the spinach wilts.

Combine Ingredients:

- In a bowl, combine the sautéed spinach, crumbled feta cheese, and chopped sun-dried tomatoes. Mix well. Season with salt and black pepper to taste.

For the Stuffed Chicken:

Preheat the Oven:

- Preheat your oven to 375°F (190°C).

Prepare Chicken Breasts:

- Make a horizontal slit along the side of each chicken breast to create a pocket without cutting all the way through.

Season Chicken:

- Season the inside of each chicken breast with salt and black pepper.

Stuff Chicken:

- Stuff each chicken breast with the spinach and feta mixture, pressing down gently to close the pocket.

Secure with Toothpicks (Optional):

- If needed, secure the opening with toothpicks to keep the filling from falling out.

Season with Herbs (Optional):
- In a small bowl, mix dried oregano, dried thyme, and dried rosemary. Season the outside of each chicken breast with the herb mixture.

Sear Chicken:
- In an oven-safe skillet, heat 1 tablespoon of olive oil over medium-high heat. Sear the stuffed chicken breasts for 2-3 minutes on each side until they develop a golden-brown crust.

Finish in the Oven:
- Transfer the skillet to the preheated oven and bake for about 20-25 minutes or until the chicken reaches an internal temperature of 165°F (74°C).

Rest and Serve:
- Remove the stuffed chicken breasts from the oven and let them rest for a few minutes before serving.

Serve:
- Serve the Spinach and Feta Stuffed Chicken Breast with your favorite side dishes.

Enjoy your delicious and flavorful Spinach and Feta Stuffed Chicken Breast! This dish is sure to impress with its savory filling and juicy chicken.

Butternut Squash Soup

Ingredients:

- 1 medium-sized butternut squash, peeled, seeded, and diced
- 1 large carrot, peeled and chopped
- 1 apple, peeled, cored, and chopped
- 1 onion, chopped
- 2 cloves garlic, minced
- 4 cups vegetable or chicken broth
- 1 teaspoon ground cinnamon
- 1/2 teaspoon ground nutmeg
- 1/2 teaspoon ground ginger
- Salt and black pepper to taste
- 2 tablespoons olive oil or butter
- 1/2 cup heavy cream or coconut milk (optional, for creaminess)
- Toasted pumpkin seeds or croutons for garnish (optional)
- Fresh parsley or chives for garnish (optional)

Instructions:

Prepare Vegetables:
- Peel, seed, and dice the butternut squash. Peel and chop the carrot. Peel, core, and chop the apple. Chop the onion and mince the garlic.

Saute Vegetables:
- In a large pot, heat olive oil or butter over medium heat. Add the chopped onion and garlic, and sauté until softened.

Add Butternut Squash, Carrot, and Apple:
- Add the diced butternut squash, chopped carrot, and apple to the pot. Cook for a few minutes, stirring occasionally.

Season:
- Sprinkle ground cinnamon, ground nutmeg, ground ginger, salt, and black pepper over the vegetables. Stir to coat evenly.

Add Broth:
- Pour in the vegetable or chicken broth, ensuring that the vegetables are fully submerged. Bring the mixture to a boil.

Simmer:
- Reduce the heat to low, cover the pot, and let the soup simmer for about 20-25 minutes or until the vegetables are tender.

Blend:
- Using an immersion blender or transferring the soup to a blender in batches, blend until smooth and creamy.

Adjust Consistency:
- If the soup is too thick, you can add more broth or water to achieve your desired consistency.

Add Cream (Optional):
- Stir in heavy cream or coconut milk for added creaminess. Adjust the seasoning to taste.

Serve:
- Ladle the Butternut Squash Soup into bowls. Garnish with toasted pumpkin seeds, croutons, fresh parsley, or chives if desired.

Enjoy:
- Serve the soup hot and enjoy its rich and comforting flavors.

This Butternut Squash Soup is not only delicious but also versatile. Feel free to customize it by adding your favorite herbs, spices, or toppings. It's a perfect dish for autumn or any time you crave a warm and satisfying soup.

Roasted Red Pepper Hummus

Ingredients:

- 1 can (15 oz) chickpeas, drained and rinsed
- 1/2 cup roasted red peppers (from a jar or homemade), drained
- 1/4 cup tahini
- 1/4 cup extra virgin olive oil
- 1 clove garlic, minced
- Juice of 1 lemon
- 1/2 teaspoon ground cumin
- 1/2 teaspoon paprika
- Salt and black pepper to taste
- Optional: Pinch of cayenne pepper for a hint of heat
- Water (as needed for desired consistency)

Instructions:

Prepare Chickpeas:
- If using canned chickpeas, drain and rinse them under cold water.

Combine Ingredients:
- In a food processor, combine chickpeas, roasted red peppers, tahini, olive oil, minced garlic, lemon juice, ground cumin, paprika, salt, black pepper, and cayenne pepper (if using).

Blend:
- Blend the ingredients until smooth. If the mixture is too thick, you can add water, one tablespoon at a time, until you reach your desired consistency.

Taste and Adjust:
- Taste the hummus and adjust the seasoning, adding more salt, pepper, or lemon juice if needed.

Serve:
- Transfer the Roasted Red Pepper Hummus to a serving bowl. Drizzle with a bit of olive oil and sprinkle with additional paprika for garnish.

Optional: Add Texture:
- For added texture, you can reserve a tablespoon of chickpeas and a teaspoon of chopped roasted red pepper. Sprinkle these on top of the hummus before serving.

Enjoy:
- Serve the Roasted Red Pepper Hummus with pita bread, crackers, vegetable sticks, or as a spread in sandwiches or wraps.

Enjoy your homemade Roasted Red Pepper Hummus as a delicious and nutritious snack or appetizer. This flavorful variation is sure to be a hit at gatherings or as a tasty addition to your daily meals.

Garlic Ginger Soy Glazed Salmon

Ingredients:

For the Salmon:

- 4 salmon fillets
- Salt and black pepper to taste
- 1 tablespoon olive oil
- Sesame seeds and chopped green onions for garnish (optional)

For the Garlic Ginger Soy Glaze:

- 3 tablespoons soy sauce
- 2 tablespoons honey or maple syrup
- 1 tablespoon fresh ginger, grated
- 3 cloves garlic, minced
- 1 tablespoon rice vinegar
- 1 teaspoon sesame oil

Instructions:

For the Garlic Ginger Soy Glaze:

Prepare Glaze:
- In a bowl, whisk together soy sauce, honey or maple syrup, grated ginger, minced garlic, rice vinegar, and sesame oil. Set aside.

For the Salmon:

Preheat Oven:
- Preheat your oven to 400°F (200°C).

Season Salmon:
- Pat the salmon fillets dry with paper towels. Season both sides with salt and black pepper.

Sear Salmon:

- In an oven-safe skillet, heat olive oil over medium-high heat. Place the salmon fillets in the skillet, skin side down if they have skin. Sear for 2-3 minutes until golden brown.

Brush with Glaze:
- Brush the top of each salmon fillet with the prepared garlic ginger soy glaze.

Transfer to Oven:
- Transfer the skillet to the preheated oven and bake for about 8-10 minutes, or until the salmon is cooked through and easily flakes with a fork.

Glaze Again (Optional):
- Optionally, you can brush the salmon with more of the glaze halfway through the baking time.

Garnish:
- Once the salmon is done, remove it from the oven and brush with additional glaze if desired. Garnish with sesame seeds and chopped green onions.

Serve:
- Serve the Garlic Ginger Soy Glazed Salmon over rice, quinoa, or your favorite side dish.

Enjoy your Garlic Ginger Soy Glazed Salmon with its sweet and savory flavors. This dish is not only delicious but also quick to prepare, making it a perfect option for a weeknight dinner. Adjust the sweetness or saltiness of the glaze according to your taste preferences.

Ratatouille

Ingredients:

- 1 large eggplant, diced
- 2 zucchinis, sliced
- 1 large bell pepper (red, yellow, or green), diced
- 1 large onion, thinly sliced
- 3 tomatoes, diced
- 4 cloves garlic, minced
- 2 tablespoons tomato paste
- 2 tablespoons olive oil
- 1 teaspoon dried thyme
- 1 teaspoon dried rosemary
- 1 teaspoon dried oregano

- Salt and black pepper to taste
- Fresh basil or parsley, chopped, for garnish

Instructions:

Prepare Vegetables:
- Dice the eggplant, slice the zucchinis, dice the bell pepper, thinly slice the onion, dice the tomatoes, and mince the garlic.

Sauté Onion and Garlic:
- In a large pot or deep skillet, heat olive oil over medium heat. Add the sliced onions and minced garlic. Sauté until the onions are softened and translucent.

Add Bell Pepper and Eggplant:
- Add the diced bell pepper and eggplant to the pot. Cook for about 5-7 minutes until the vegetables start to soften.

Add Zucchini:
- Stir in the sliced zucchinis and cook for an additional 5 minutes until they begin to soften.

Add Tomatoes and Tomato Paste:
- Add the diced tomatoes and tomato paste to the pot. Stir well to combine.

Season:
- Season the mixture with dried thyme, dried rosemary, dried oregano, salt, and black pepper. Stir to evenly distribute the seasonings.

Simmer:
- Reduce the heat to low, cover the pot, and let the Ratatouille simmer for about 20-25 minutes or until all the vegetables are tender. Stir occasionally.

Adjust Seasoning:
- Taste and adjust the seasoning if needed. You can add more salt, pepper, or herbs according to your taste.

Garnish:
- Once the Ratatouille is done, garnish it with chopped fresh basil or parsley.

Serve:
- Serve the Ratatouille warm as a side dish or as a main course over rice, quinoa, or crusty bread.

Enjoy your homemade Ratatouille, a flavorful and hearty dish that celebrates the vibrant flavors of fresh vegetables. It's a great way to showcase the abundance of summer produce in a delicious and satisfying way.

Edamame and Avocado Salad

Ingredients:

For the Salad:

- 2 cups shelled edamame (cooked and cooled)
- 2 ripe avocados, diced
- 1 cup cherry tomatoes, halved
- 1/4 cup red onion, finely chopped
- 1/4 cup fresh cilantro or parsley, chopped

For the Dressing:

- 2 tablespoons olive oil
- 1 tablespoon lime juice
- 1 tablespoon soy sauce
- 1 clove garlic, minced
- 1 teaspoon honey or maple syrup (optional)
- Salt and black pepper to taste

Instructions:

For the Salad:

Prepare Edamame:
- If using frozen edamame, cook according to package instructions. If using fresh edamame, blanch in boiling water for about 5 minutes, then rinse with cold water to cool.

Combine Ingredients:
- In a large salad bowl, combine the cooled edamame, diced avocados, halved cherry tomatoes, chopped red onion, and cilantro or parsley.

For the Dressing:

Prepare Dressing:

- In a small bowl, whisk together olive oil, lime juice, soy sauce, minced garlic, honey or maple syrup (if using), salt, and black pepper.

Toss Salad:
- Pour the dressing over the salad ingredients. Gently toss the salad until all ingredients are well coated with the dressing.

Chill (Optional):
- Refrigerate the Edamame and Avocado Salad for about 30 minutes before serving to allow the flavors to meld. This step is optional but enhances the taste.

Serve:
- Serve the salad chilled as a side dish or a light and refreshing main course.

Enjoy your Edamame and Avocado Salad! This dish is not only vibrant and flavorful but also packed with protein and healthy fats. It's perfect for a quick and nutritious meal, and you can easily customize it by adding other ingredients like cucumber, bell peppers, or your favorite herbs.

Cauliflower Buffalo Bites

Ingredients:

For the Cauliflower Bites:

- 1 large head of cauliflower, cut into bite-sized florets
- 1 cup all-purpose flour (or chickpea flour for a gluten-free option)
- 1 cup milk (or plant-based milk for a vegan option)
- 1 teaspoon garlic powder
- 1 teaspoon onion powder
- 1/2 teaspoon smoked paprika
- Salt and black pepper to taste

For the Buffalo Sauce:

- 1/2 cup hot sauce (such as Frank's RedHot)
- 1/4 cup unsalted butter (or vegan butter for a vegan option)
- 1 tablespoon apple cider vinegar
- 1/2 teaspoon garlic powder
- 1/2 teaspoon Worcestershire sauce (optional, omit for a vegetarian/vegan version)

Instructions:

For the Cauliflower Bites:

Preheat Oven:
- Preheat your oven to 450°F (230°C). Line a baking sheet with parchment paper.

Prepare Batter:
- In a bowl, whisk together the flour, milk, garlic powder, onion powder, smoked paprika, salt, and black pepper until you have a smooth batter.

Coat Cauliflower:
- Dip each cauliflower floret into the batter, allowing any excess to drip off. Place the coated cauliflower on the prepared baking sheet.

Bake:
- Bake in the preheated oven for about 20-25 minutes, or until the cauliflower is golden brown and crispy. You can flip the cauliflower halfway through the baking time for even crispiness.

For the Buffalo Sauce:

Prepare Buffalo Sauce:
- In a saucepan over low heat, melt the butter. Add the hot sauce, apple cider vinegar, garlic powder, and Worcestershire sauce (if using). Stir until well combined and heated through. Adjust the heat level to your liking.

Coat Cauliflower in Buffalo Sauce:
- Once the cauliflower bites are done baking, transfer them to a large bowl. Pour the buffalo sauce over the cauliflower and toss until all the pieces are well coated.

Serve:
- Serve the Cauliflower Buffalo Bites with your favorite dipping sauce and celery sticks. Ranch or blue cheese dressing is a classic choice.

Enjoy your Cauliflower Buffalo Bites as a delicious and satisfying appetizer or snack. These bites are perfect for parties, game nights, or whenever you're craving a spicy and flavorful treat.

Thai Coconut Curry Noodles

Ingredients:

- 8 oz rice noodles or any noodles of your choice
- 1 tablespoon vegetable oil
- 1 onion, thinly sliced
- 2 bell peppers, thinly sliced (use a mix of colors)
- 2 carrots, julienned or thinly sliced

- 3 cloves garlic, minced
- 1 tablespoon red curry paste
- 1 can (14 oz) coconut milk
- 1 tablespoon soy sauce
- 1 tablespoon brown sugar or palm sugar
- 1 tablespoon lime juice
- 1 cup broccoli florets (optional)
- 1 cup sliced mushrooms (optional)
- Fresh cilantro and lime wedges for garnish

Instructions:

Prepare Noodles:
- Cook the noodles according to package instructions. Drain and set aside.

Sauté Vegetables:
- In a large pan or wok, heat the vegetable oil over medium-high heat. Add the sliced onion, bell peppers, and carrots. Stir-fry for 3-4 minutes until the vegetables are slightly softened.

Add Garlic and Curry Paste:
- Add minced garlic to the pan and stir for about 30 seconds until fragrant. Add the red curry paste and continue to stir for another minute.

Pour Coconut Milk:
- Pour in the coconut milk, soy sauce, and brown sugar (or palm sugar). Stir well to combine and bring the mixture to a simmer.

Add Lime Juice:
- Add lime juice to the curry mixture and stir.

Add Broccoli and Mushrooms (Optional):
- If using broccoli and mushrooms, add them to the pan and cook for an additional 3-4 minutes until the vegetables are tender.

Combine with Noodles:
- Add the cooked and drained noodles to the pan. Toss the noodles in the curry sauce until they are well coated.

Adjust Seasoning:
- Taste and adjust the seasoning. You can add more soy sauce, lime juice, or curry paste according to your preference.

Serve:
- Serve the Thai Coconut Curry Noodles hot, garnished with fresh cilantro and lime wedges.

Enjoy your Thai Coconut Curry Noodles, a delicious and satisfying meal with the perfect balance of creamy coconut, spicy curry, and tender noodles. Feel free to customize the vegetables and spice level to suit your taste.

Bruschetta with Fresh Basil

Ingredients:

- 4-5 ripe tomatoes, diced
- 1-2 cloves garlic, minced
- 1/4 cup fresh basil, chopped
- 2 tablespoons extra virgin olive oil
- 1 teaspoon balsamic vinegar (optional)
- Salt and black pepper to taste
- Baguette or Italian bread, sliced
- Optional: Balsamic glaze for drizzling

Instructions:

Prepare Tomatoes:
- Dice the ripe tomatoes and place them in a bowl.

Add Garlic and Basil:
- Add the minced garlic and chopped fresh basil to the diced tomatoes.

Drizzle Olive Oil:
- Drizzle extra virgin olive oil over the tomato mixture.

Optional Balsamic Vinegar:
- If using, add balsamic vinegar to the mixture for an extra layer of flavor.

Season:
- Season the bruschetta with salt and black pepper to taste. Toss everything gently to combine.

Let It Marinate:
- Allow the bruschetta mixture to marinate for at least 15-20 minutes, allowing the flavors to meld.

Slice and Toast Bread:
- Slice the baguette or Italian bread into 1/2-inch thick slices. Toast the slices either on a grill, in the oven, or on a stovetop grilling pan until they are golden and crispy.

Assemble:

- Just before serving, spoon the tomato mixture generously onto each toasted bread slice.

Optional Drizzle:
- Optionally, drizzle a little balsamic glaze over the top for added sweetness and presentation.

Serve:
- Serve the bruschetta with fresh basil immediately, and enjoy the burst of flavors.

Bruschetta with fresh basil is a perfect appetizer for summer or any occasion when tomatoes are at their peak. It's a simple yet elegant dish that showcases the vibrant and fresh flavors of the ingredients.

Shrimp and Vegetable Skewers

Ingredients:

For the Marinade:

- 1/4 cup olive oil
- 2 tablespoons fresh lemon juice
- 2 cloves garlic, minced
- 1 teaspoon dried oregano
- 1 teaspoon paprika
- Salt and black pepper to taste

For the Skewers:

- 1 pound large shrimp, peeled and deveined
- Cherry tomatoes
- Bell peppers, cut into chunks
- Red onion, cut into chunks
- Zucchini, sliced
- Wooden or metal skewers (if using wooden, soak them in water for at least 30 minutes)

Optional for Serving:

- Lemon wedges
- Fresh parsley, chopped

Instructions:

Prepare Marinade:
- In a bowl, whisk together olive oil, fresh lemon juice, minced garlic, dried oregano, paprika, salt, and black pepper.

Marinate Shrimp:
- Place the peeled and deveined shrimp in a shallow dish. Pour half of the marinade over the shrimp and toss to coat evenly. Allow the shrimp to marinate for at least 15-20 minutes.

Prepare Vegetables:
- While the shrimp is marinating, prepare the vegetables by cutting them into chunks or slices.

Assemble Skewers:
- Thread the marinated shrimp, cherry tomatoes, bell pepper chunks, red onion chunks, and zucchini slices onto the skewers, alternating between shrimp and vegetables.

Brush with Marinade:
- Brush the assembled skewers with the remaining marinade.

Preheat Grill:
- Preheat the grill to medium-high heat.

Grill Skewers:
- Grill the skewers for 2-3 minutes per side, or until the shrimp are opaque and cooked through. The vegetables should be slightly charred and tender.

Serve:
- Remove the skewers from the grill and transfer them to a serving platter. Optionally, garnish with chopped fresh parsley and serve with lemon wedges on the side.

Enjoy:
- Serve the shrimp and vegetable skewers immediately, either as an appetizer or a main dish. They pair well with rice, couscous, or a fresh salad.

These shrimp and vegetable skewers are not only visually appealing but also full of vibrant flavors. The combination of grilled shrimp and colorful veggies makes for a delightful and healthy meal.

Roasted Sweet Potato Wedges

Ingredients:

- 2 large sweet potatoes, washed and scrubbed
- 2 tablespoons olive oil
- 1 teaspoon paprika
- 1 teaspoon garlic powder
- 1 teaspoon dried thyme (optional)
- Salt and black pepper to taste
- Optional: Fresh parsley, chopped, for garnish

Instructions:

Preheat the Oven:
- Preheat your oven to 425°F (220°C).

Prepare the Sweet Potatoes:
- Cut the sweet potatoes into wedges. You can leave the skin on for added texture and nutrients.

Coat with Olive Oil and Seasonings:
- In a large bowl, toss the sweet potato wedges with olive oil, paprika, garlic powder, dried thyme (if using), salt, and black pepper. Make sure the wedges are evenly coated.

Arrange on Baking Sheet:
- Arrange the seasoned sweet potato wedges in a single layer on a baking sheet lined with parchment paper. This helps prevent sticking and makes cleanup easier.

Roast in the Oven:
- Roast the sweet potato wedges in the preheated oven for 25-30 minutes, or until they are golden brown and tender. Flip them halfway through the roasting time for even cooking.

Garnish (Optional):
- If desired, garnish the roasted sweet potato wedges with chopped fresh parsley for a burst of color and freshness.

Serve:
- Serve the roasted sweet potato wedges hot as a side dish or snack. They pair well with various dipping sauces such as garlic aioli, ketchup, or a yogurt-based dip.

These roasted sweet potato wedges are a delightful combination of crispy on the outside and tender on the inside. They make a tasty and nutritious addition to your meals, providing a natural sweetness and plenty of vitamins and fiber.

Caprese Quinoa Bowl

Ingredients:

For the Quinoa Bowl:

- 1 cup quinoa, rinsed
- 2 cups cherry tomatoes, halved
- 1 cup fresh mozzarella balls or cubes
- 1/2 cup fresh basil leaves, torn
- Balsamic glaze for drizzling
- Salt and black pepper to taste

For the Balsamic Vinaigrette:

- 1/4 cup balsamic vinegar
- 1/3 cup extra-virgin olive oil
- 1 tablespoon Dijon mustard
- 1 clove garlic, minced
- Salt and black pepper to taste

Instructions:

For the Quinoa Bowl:

Cook Quinoa:
- In a medium saucepan, combine quinoa with 2 cups of water. Bring to a boil, then reduce heat to low, cover, and simmer for about 15 minutes or until the quinoa is cooked and water is absorbed. Fluff with a fork.

Assemble Bowl:
- In serving bowls, layer cooked quinoa, cherry tomatoes, fresh mozzarella, and torn basil leaves.

Season:
- Season the bowl with salt and black pepper to taste.

For the Balsamic Vinaigrette:

Prepare Vinaigrette:
- In a small bowl, whisk together balsamic vinegar, extra-virgin olive oil, Dijon mustard, minced garlic, salt, and black pepper until well combined.

Drizzle Over Bowl:
- Drizzle the balsamic vinaigrette over the Caprese quinoa bowl.

Finish with Balsamic Glaze:
- Finish the bowl by drizzling balsamic glaze over the top for added sweetness and presentation.

Serve:
- Serve the Caprese Quinoa Bowl immediately, and enjoy the combination of flavors and textures.

This Caprese Quinoa Bowl is a satisfying and nutritious meal, providing a good balance of protein from quinoa and mozzarella, along with the freshness of tomatoes and basil. The balsamic vinaigrette and glaze add a tangy and sweet touch to elevate the dish.
Lemon Dijon Baked Chicken

Ingredients:

- 4 boneless, skinless chicken breasts
- 1/4 cup Dijon mustard
- 3 tablespoons fresh lemon juice
- 2 tablespoons olive oil
- 2 cloves garlic, minced
- 1 teaspoon dried thyme
- 1 teaspoon dried rosemary
- Salt and black pepper to taste
- Lemon slices for garnish (optional)
- Fresh parsley, chopped, for garnish (optional)

Instructions:

Preheat Oven:
- Preheat your oven to 400°F (200°C).

Prepare Chicken:
- Pat the chicken breasts dry with paper towels and place them in a baking dish.

Prepare Marinade:
- In a bowl, whisk together Dijon mustard, fresh lemon juice, olive oil, minced garlic, dried thyme, dried rosemary, salt, and black pepper.

Coat Chicken:
- Pour the marinade over the chicken breasts, ensuring they are well coated on all sides. You can use a brush or your hands to evenly distribute the marinade.

Marinate:
- Allow the chicken to marinate for at least 30 minutes to let the flavors infuse. For a more intense flavor, you can marinate it longer in the refrigerator.

Bake:
- Bake the chicken in the preheated oven for approximately 25-30 minutes or until the internal temperature reaches 165°F (74°C). The exact cooking time may vary depending on the thickness of the chicken breasts.

Broil (Optional):
- If you want a golden brown finish, you can broil the chicken for an additional 2-3 minutes at the end of the cooking time.

Garnish:
- Garnish the Lemon Dijon Baked Chicken with lemon slices and chopped fresh parsley, if desired.

Serve:
- Serve the chicken hot, accompanied by your favorite sides such as roasted vegetables, rice, or a fresh salad.

Enjoy your Lemon Dijon Baked Chicken, a dish that's both light and flavorful. The combination of tangy Dijon mustard and bright lemon creates a delightful marinade for the chicken, making it a perfect option for a quick and tasty meal.

Roasted Beet and Goat Cheese Salad

Ingredients:

For the Salad:

- 3 medium-sized beets, washed and trimmed
- 5 cups mixed salad greens (arugula, spinach, or your choice)
- 1/2 cup crumbled goat cheese
- 1/4 cup walnuts, toasted and chopped

- Salt and black pepper to taste

For the Dressing:

- 3 tablespoons balsamic vinegar
- 1/4 cup extra-virgin olive oil
- 1 tablespoon Dijon mustard
- 1 teaspoon honey
- Salt and black pepper to taste

Instructions:

For the Roasted Beets:

Preheat Oven:
- Preheat your oven to 400°F (200°C).

Roast Beets:
- Wrap each beet in aluminum foil and place them on a baking sheet. Roast in the preheated oven for about 45-60 minutes, or until the beets are tender when pierced with a fork.

Cool and Peel:
- Allow the roasted beets to cool. Once cool enough to handle, peel the skin off using your hands or a knife. Cut the beets into bite-sized wedges or slices.

For the Dressing:

Prepare Dressing:
- In a small bowl, whisk together balsamic vinegar, extra-virgin olive oil, Dijon mustard, honey, salt, and black pepper until well combined.

Assembling the Salad:

Prepare Salad Greens:
- In a large bowl, toss the mixed salad greens with a portion of the prepared dressing. Add more dressing to taste.

Arrange Beets and Toppings:
- Arrange the roasted beet wedges over the dressed salad greens. Sprinkle crumbled goat cheese and toasted, chopped walnuts on top.

Season:
- Season the salad with salt and black pepper to taste.

Serve:

- Serve the Roasted Beet and Goat Cheese Salad immediately, drizzling extra dressing if desired.

Enjoy this colorful and flavorful salad as a refreshing appetizer or a light and nutritious main course. The combination of sweet roasted beets, tangy goat cheese, and crunchy walnuts creates a harmonious blend of textures and tastes.

Quinoa-Stuffed Acorn Squash

Ingredients:

For the Stuffed Acorn Squash:

- 2 acorn squash, halved and seeds removed
- 1 cup quinoa, rinsed
- 2 cups vegetable broth or water
- 1 tablespoon olive oil
- 1 small onion, finely chopped
- 2 cloves garlic, minced
- 1 celery stalk, finely chopped
- 1 carrot, finely chopped
- 1/2 cup dried cranberries or raisins
- 1/2 cup chopped pecans or walnuts (optional)
- 1 teaspoon dried thyme
- 1 teaspoon dried sage
- Salt and black pepper to taste

For the Maple Glaze (Optional):

- 2 tablespoons maple syrup
- 1 tablespoon olive oil
- Salt and black pepper to taste

Instructions:

For the Stuffed Acorn Squash:

Preheat Oven:
- Preheat your oven to 400°F (200°C).

Prepare Acorn Squash:

- Cut the acorn squash in half and scoop out the seeds. Place the squash halves on a baking sheet, cut side up.

Roast Squash:
- Roast the acorn squash in the preheated oven for about 30-40 minutes or until they are tender and easily pierced with a fork.

Cook Quinoa:
- While the squash is roasting, rinse the quinoa under cold water. In a saucepan, combine quinoa and vegetable broth or water. Bring to a boil, then reduce the heat, cover, and simmer for 15-20 minutes or until the quinoa is cooked and liquid is absorbed.

Sauté Vegetables:
- In a skillet, heat olive oil over medium heat. Add chopped onion, minced garlic, celery, and carrot. Sauté until the vegetables are softened.

Combine Quinoa and Vegetables:
- Combine the cooked quinoa with the sautéed vegetables. Stir in dried cranberries or raisins, chopped nuts (if using), dried thyme, dried sage, salt, and black pepper.

Stuff Acorn Squash:
- Once the acorn squash is roasted and tender, stuff each half with the quinoa and vegetable mixture.

For the Maple Glaze (Optional):

Prepare Glaze:
- In a small bowl, whisk together maple syrup, olive oil, salt, and black pepper.

Brush Glaze:
- Brush the tops of the stuffed acorn squash with the maple glaze.

Broil (Optional):
- Place the stuffed acorn squash under the broiler for 2-3 minutes or until the tops are golden brown and caramelized.

Serve:
- Serve the Quinoa-Stuffed Acorn Squash hot, optionally garnished with additional dried cranberries, chopped nuts, or fresh herbs.

This dish makes for a satisfying and visually appealing main course, showcasing the fall flavors of acorn squash and the protein-rich quinoa. The addition of a sweet maple glaze adds a delightful touch to the overall taste.

Balsamic Glazed Brussels Sprouts

Ingredients:

- 1 pound Brussels sprouts, trimmed and halved
- 2 tablespoons olive oil
- 2 tablespoons balsamic vinegar
- 1 tablespoon honey or maple syrup
- 2 cloves garlic, minced
- Salt and black pepper to taste
- Optional: Crushed red pepper flakes for a bit of heat
- Optional: Grated Parmesan cheese for serving

Instructions:

Preheat Oven:
- Preheat your oven to 400°F (200°C).

Prepare Brussels Sprouts:
- Trim the ends of the Brussels sprouts and cut them in half. If some are larger, you can quarter them for more even cooking.

Prepare Balsamic Glaze:
- In a small bowl, whisk together balsamic vinegar, honey or maple syrup, minced garlic, salt, black pepper, and crushed red pepper flakes if using.

Coat Brussels Sprouts:
- Place the halved Brussels sprouts in a large mixing bowl. Drizzle olive oil over them and toss to coat evenly.

Roast Brussels Sprouts:
- Spread the Brussels sprouts in a single layer on a baking sheet lined with parchment paper. Roast in the preheated oven for 20-25 minutes or until they are golden brown and crispy on the edges, stirring once halfway through.

Glaze Brussels Sprouts:
- In the last 5 minutes of roasting, drizzle the balsamic glaze over the Brussels sprouts and toss to coat. Continue roasting until the glaze has thickened slightly.

Serve:
- Remove the Brussels sprouts from the oven and transfer them to a serving dish. Optionally, sprinkle with grated Parmesan cheese before serving.

Enjoy:
- Serve the Balsamic Glazed Brussels Sprouts hot as a delicious and flavorful side dish.

This dish is a fantastic way to enjoy Brussels sprouts, as the roasting process caramelizes the edges, and the balsamic glaze adds a sweet and tangy flavor. It's a perfect side for holiday meals or any dinner occasion.

Tomato Basil Mozzarella Skewers

Ingredients:

- Cherry tomatoes
- Fresh mozzarella balls (bocconcini or small mozzarella pearls)
- Fresh basil leaves
- Balsamic glaze (store-bought or homemade)
- Extra-virgin olive oil
- Salt and black pepper to taste
- Optional: Wooden or metal skewers for assembling

Instructions:

Prepare Ingredients:
- Wash the cherry tomatoes and basil leaves. If using larger mozzarella balls, cut them into bite-sized pieces.

Assemble Skewers:
- Assemble the skewers by threading a cherry tomato, a folded basil leaf, and a mozzarella ball onto each skewer. Repeat until you have the desired number of skewers.

Arrange Skewers:
- Arrange the assembled skewers on a serving platter.

Season:
- Drizzle extra-virgin olive oil over the skewers. Sprinkle with salt and black pepper to taste.

Balsamic Glaze:
- Drizzle balsamic glaze over the Tomato Basil Mozzarella Skewers for added sweetness and flavor.

Serve:
- Serve the skewers immediately as a fresh and flavorful appetizer.

The Tomato Basil Mozzarella Skewers are not only visually appealing but also a delightful combination of flavors. The sweetness of the tomatoes, the aromatic basil, and the creamy mozzarella create a perfect harmony. The balsamic glaze adds a tangy and slightly sweet finish to the dish. This appetizer is perfect for gatherings, picnics, or as a light starter for any meal.

Mediterranean Couscous Salad

Ingredients:

For the Salad:

- 1 cup couscous
- 1 1/4 cups vegetable broth or water
- 1 cup cherry tomatoes, halved
- 1 cucumber, diced
- 1/2 red bell pepper, diced
- 1/2 yellow bell pepper, diced
- 1/4 red onion, finely chopped
- 1/2 cup Kalamata olives, sliced
- 1/2 cup crumbled feta cheese
- Fresh parsley, chopped, for garnish

For the Dressing:

- 1/4 cup extra-virgin olive oil
- 2 tablespoons red wine vinegar
- 1 teaspoon Dijon mustard
- 1 clove garlic, minced
- 1 teaspoon dried oregano
- Salt and black pepper to taste

Instructions:

For the Salad:

Cook Couscous:
- In a medium saucepan, bring vegetable broth or water to a boil. Stir in couscous, cover, and remove from heat. Let it sit for 5 minutes, then fluff with a fork.

Prepare Vegetables:

- In a large mixing bowl, combine the cooked couscous with cherry tomatoes, cucumber, red bell pepper, yellow bell pepper, red onion, Kalamata olives, and crumbled feta cheese.

For the Dressing:

Prepare Dressing:
- In a small bowl, whisk together extra-virgin olive oil, red wine vinegar, Dijon mustard, minced garlic, dried oregano, salt, and black pepper.

Combine Salad and Dressing:
- Pour the dressing over the couscous and vegetable mixture. Toss everything together until well coated.

Chill (Optional):
- Refrigerate the Mediterranean Couscous Salad for at least 30 minutes to allow the flavors to meld. This step is optional, and you can also serve it immediately.

Garnish:
- Garnish the salad with freshly chopped parsley before serving.

Serve:
- Serve the Mediterranean Couscous Salad as a side dish or a light and refreshing main course.

This salad is not only flavorful but also versatile. Feel free to customize it by adding other Mediterranean ingredients like artichoke hearts, sun-dried tomatoes, or roasted red peppers. It's perfect for picnics, barbecues, or as a healthy and satisfying lunch.

Garlic Butter Shrimp and Broccoli

Ingredients:

- 1 pound large shrimp, peeled and deveined
- 3 cups broccoli florets
- 4 tablespoons unsalted butter
- 4 cloves garlic, minced
- 1 teaspoon paprika
- 1/2 teaspoon red pepper flakes (optional, for heat)
- Salt and black pepper to taste
- 2 tablespoons fresh lemon juice
- Fresh parsley, chopped, for garnish

Instructions:

Prepare Shrimp and Broccoli:
- Pat the shrimp dry with paper towels and season with salt, black pepper, and paprika. Set aside. Cut the broccoli into bite-sized florets.

Cook Broccoli:
- Steam or blanch the broccoli in boiling water for 2-3 minutes or until it is just tender. Drain and set aside.

Cook Shrimp:
- In a large skillet over medium-high heat, melt 2 tablespoons of butter. Add the seasoned shrimp to the skillet and cook for 1-2 minutes per side or until they turn pink. Remove the shrimp from the skillet and set aside.

Make Garlic Butter Sauce:
- In the same skillet, add the remaining 2 tablespoons of butter. Add minced garlic and cook for about 1 minute until fragrant. If using red pepper flakes for heat, add them at this stage.

Combine Shrimp, Broccoli, and Sauce:
- Return the cooked shrimp to the skillet and add the steamed broccoli. Toss everything together to coat in the garlic butter sauce.

Add Lemon Juice:
- Squeeze fresh lemon juice over the shrimp and broccoli mixture. Adjust salt and pepper to taste.

Garnish and Serve:
- Garnish with chopped fresh parsley for a burst of freshness. Serve the Garlic Butter Shrimp and Broccoli immediately.

This dish is perfect for a quick weeknight dinner or when you want a flavorful and light meal. The garlic butter sauce adds richness, and the combination of shrimp and broccoli provides a healthy and satisfying balance. You can serve it over rice, pasta, or with a side of crusty bread to soak up the delicious sauce.

Kale and White Bean Soup

Ingredients:

- 1 tablespoon olive oil
- 1 onion, finely chopped
- 2 carrots, peeled and diced
- 2 celery stalks, diced
- 3 cloves garlic, minced

- 1 teaspoon dried thyme
- 1 teaspoon dried rosemary
- 1 bay leaf
- 4 cups vegetable broth
- 2 cans (15 ounces each) white beans (cannellini or Great Northern), drained and rinsed
- 1 bunch kale, stems removed and leaves chopped
- Salt and black pepper to taste
- 1 tablespoon lemon juice (optional)
- Grated Parmesan cheese for serving (optional)

Instructions:

Sauté Vegetables:
- In a large pot or Dutch oven, heat the olive oil over medium heat. Add the chopped onion, carrots, and celery. Sauté until the vegetables are softened, about 5 minutes.

Add Garlic and Herbs:
- Add the minced garlic, dried thyme, dried rosemary, and bay leaf. Cook for an additional 1-2 minutes until the garlic is fragrant.

Pour Broth:
- Pour in the vegetable broth and bring the mixture to a simmer.

Add White Beans:
- Add the drained and rinsed white beans to the pot. Simmer for about 10 minutes to allow the flavors to meld.

Add Kale:
- Stir in the chopped kale leaves. Cook for an additional 5-7 minutes or until the kale is wilted and tender.

Season:
- Season the soup with salt and black pepper to taste. If desired, add lemon juice for a hint of brightness.

Serve:
- Remove the bay leaf. Ladle the Kale and White Bean Soup into bowls and serve hot.

Optional: Garnish with Parmesan:
- Optionally, garnish each serving with grated Parmesan cheese for added flavor.

This Kale and White Bean Soup is not only delicious but also a great source of fiber, vitamins, and minerals. It's a comforting and wholesome soup that can be enjoyed on its own or with a side of crusty bread. Perfect for a cozy evening meal or as a nutritious lunch option.

Ginger Sesame Tofu Stir-Fry

Ingredients:

For the Tofu:

- 1 block extra-firm tofu, pressed and cubed
- 2 tablespoons soy sauce
- 1 tablespoon sesame oil
- 1 tablespoon cornstarch
- 1 tablespoon vegetable oil (for frying)

For the Stir-Fry:

- 1 tablespoon vegetable oil
- 1 tablespoon fresh ginger, minced
- 3 cloves garlic, minced
- 1 bell pepper, thinly sliced
- 1 cup broccoli florets
- 1 carrot, julienned
- 1 zucchini, sliced
- 2 tablespoons soy sauce
- 1 tablespoon rice vinegar
- 1 tablespoon sesame oil
- 1 tablespoon honey or maple syrup
- 1 tablespoon sesame seeds (for garnish)
- Green onions, chopped (for garnish)
- Cooked rice or noodles (for serving)

Instructions:

For the Tofu:

　　Press Tofu:

- Press the tofu to remove excess water. Cut it into cubes.

Marinate Tofu:
- In a bowl, combine soy sauce, sesame oil, and cornstarch. Add the tofu cubes to the marinade, ensuring they are well coated. Let it marinate for at least 15-30 minutes.

Pan-Fry Tofu:
- Heat vegetable oil in a skillet over medium-high heat. Add the marinated tofu cubes and cook until they are golden brown on all sides. Remove from the pan and set aside.

For the Stir-Fry:

Prepare Vegetables:
- In the same skillet, add 1 tablespoon of vegetable oil. Add minced ginger and garlic. Sauté for about 1 minute until fragrant.

Add Vegetables:
- Add sliced bell pepper, broccoli florets, julienned carrot, and sliced zucchini to the skillet. Stir-fry for 3-4 minutes until the vegetables are tender-crisp.

Make Stir-Fry Sauce:
- In a small bowl, whisk together soy sauce, rice vinegar, sesame oil, and honey or maple syrup.

Combine Tofu and Vegetables:
- Add the cooked tofu back to the skillet. Pour the stir-fry sauce over the tofu and vegetables. Toss everything together until well coated and heated through.

Garnish and Serve:
- Garnish with sesame seeds and chopped green onions. Serve the Ginger Sesame Tofu Stir-Fry over cooked rice or noodles.

Enjoy this flavorful and satisfying Ginger Sesame Tofu Stir-Fry as a wholesome and plant-based meal. The combination of ginger, sesame, and savory tofu makes it a delightful option for a quick and tasty dinner.